31 Unique Ways to Monetize Your Book

WORKBOOK

By Kelly Falardeau

This book has been written with the help of AI.

ISBN: 978-1-989849-40-8

Exercise for Module 3
The Grand Book Makeover

Here's a practical, hands-on exercise that will make your book go from drab to fab! We're going to create a "Book Attractiveness Blueprint" together. You'll need a pen, a notebook, and a generous sprinkle of creativity.

1. Draw Your Dream Cover: Don't worry, you don't need to be the next Picasso for this. Simply draw a sketch of what you'd like your book cover to look like. Include colors, images, and any other elements that you think would make it pop.

2. Title Brainstorm: Write down at least 10 possible titles for your book. Go wild with it, the crazier, the better. This is not the time to be shy! Remember, we're aiming for catchy and memorable.

3. Subheading Sweepstakes: Write down 5 potential subtitles for your book. Your subtitle should hint at what the book's about and how it can benefit the reader.

4. Craft Your Hook: In one paragraph, write a book description that would make anyone eager to read your book. Think of it as a movie trailer - give just enough to intrigue, but not enough to give away the whole plot.

5. Interior Design Plans: Make a list of 5 ideas on how you can make the inside of your book as appealing as the cover. Consider formatting, fonts, images, or even splashes of color.

6. Bonus Content Bonanza: List down 5 types of bonus content you could include in your book. Could you add interviews, a sneak peek of your next book, exclusive insights, or personal notes to your readers?

After you've completed this exercise, take a step back and look at your creation. This, my friend, is the first draft of your Book Attractiveness Blueprint. It should give you a clearer vision of what you want your book to look like and how it can stand out from the crowd.

Remember, in the bustling marketplace of books, your book is not just competing against other books in your genre, it's competing against every book out there. By making your book as attractive as possible, you increase the odds of it being picked up by browsing readers.

Now, off you go! Enjoy the process, and remember to have fun with it!

NOTES:

Exercise for Module 4
Choose Your Format Adventure

For this exercise, we're going on an adventure! No, not a trek in the Himalayas, but rather a journey to explore the best format for your book. Your mission, should you choose to accept it, is to dive deep into your reader's shoes and explore your book from their perspective. Let's call it "Operation Reader Empathy".

Step 1: Reader Profile

Think of your ideal reader. Let's give them a name and a face. Imagine what their day looks like. Are they constantly on the move, multitasking? Or are they more of the laid-back, tea-in-the-garden-with-a-book kind of person? Write a short profile of your reader, focusing on their lifestyle and reading habits.

Step 2: Format Matching

Now that you have your reader in mind, let's match them with the best format. Would they love an eBook they can carry everywhere on their device? Or a Paperback to display on their shelf? Maybe they would appreciate an Audiobook to listen to during their commute? Write down the format that you think matches your reader's profile and explain why.

Step 3: Shopping Experience

Put yourself in your reader's shoes and take a trip to your imaginary online store. Imagine you're them, coming across your book for the first time. Which format would catch their eye first? Which one would they click on? Try to visualize the buying process from their perspective.

Step 4: Bundle Bonanza

Now, let's think about bundles. If you offered your book in all three formats as a bundle, would your reader be interested? Would they appreciate the discount and the variety? Or would they prefer to stick to one format? Remember, the goal here is not to push all formats, but to understand what would appeal to your reader the most.

Step 5: Feedback Loop

Finally, after your reader has read your book, would they be willing to leave a review? How can the format of your book make it easier for them to do so? For instance, eBooks often have direct links to review platforms, making the process easier. Consider how your chosen format can encourage readers to engage with you beyond just reading your book.

Once you've completed this exercise, you should have a clear idea of which formats would work best for your book and your reader. Remember, in the end, it's all about ensuring that your readers have the best possible experience with your literary masterpiece. Happy adventuring!

NOTES:

Exercise for Module 5
Mastering the Online Teaching Trifecta

This exercise is all about discovering the potential of your book as an online course, workshop, and webinar. Let's think of it as a game show called "Monetization Mania". No, there aren't any glittering sequins, over-enthusiastic hosts, or dramatic music, but I promise you'll have fun (and gain some insightful knowledge too!).

Step 1: The Course Conundrum

Imagine your book is a contestant on a cooking show. Your challenge is to break down your book into a 5-course meal, each course representing a key lesson or concept from your book. What would each course look like? Is it a hearty main course or a light appetizer? How would you present it to make it appealing? Write down the 'menu' of your 5-course book-meal.

Step 2: Workshop Wonders

For this round, you're an interior designer. Your task is to design a virtual room where you'll conduct your workshop. What does it look like? What tools or features would it have to make the learning experience engaging and memorable? Sketch out the room and note down its features.

Step 3: Webinar Whirlwind

Now, you're a talk show host. Plan out your dream webinar episode based on your book. Who would be your guest speaker? What topics would you cover? What fun or engaging segments would you include? Jot down the script outline for your talk show episode.

Step 4: Feedback Fiesta

Lastly, let's not forget about your audience! Think of ways you could get feedback from your course students, workshop attendees, and webinar viewers. How would you encourage them to share their thoughts, suggestions, and testimonials? Write down at least 3 strategies you could use.

And there you have it! You're now a bard, a knight, and a round table facilitator. This exercise should not only make you giggle but also give you some tangible starting points to consider when planning your speaking gigs or consultation sessions. Remember, humor can be a fantastic tool to engage your audience. So, keep the fun alive as you embark on your speaking and consulting adventures!

NOTES:

Exercise for Module 7
Fashioning Your Bookish Merchandise

This exercise is designed to help you identify and design potential merchandise for your book. Let's unleash your inner fashion designer and product creator!

Step 1: The Quotable Quotes

List down five powerful, impactful, or witty quotes from your book that would look fantastic on a piece of merchandise. These could be key takeaways, punchlines, or thought-provoking statements.

Step 2: The Merchandise Matchmaker

Pair each quote with a piece of merchandise that you think it would suit perfectly. A motivational quote might be a good fit for a poster or a mug, while a punchline might work well on a T-shirt or a hat. Feel free to think outside the box!

Step 3: The Sketchy Details

Now it's time to sketch! Design a rough concept for each merchandise-quote pair. Don't worry if you're not an artist - these are just preliminary ideas to get the ball rolling.

Step 4: The Cost-Benefit Analyst

For each merchandise-quote pair, jot down a potential selling price and any costs associated with its creation (you can research this online). This will give you an initial idea of the profitability of each item.

Step 5: The Market Surveyor

Finally, pick your favorite merchandise-quote pair and share the concept with a small group of your target audience. Gather feedback on the design, the quote, and the price.

This step will give you valuable insights into whether your idea has a market.

This fun exercise should kickstart your creative process and help you see the potential of your book as more than just a reading material, but a brand. So, start thinking, sketching, and surveying – your readers are waiting for your bookish merchandise!

Check out my store which has my collection of art project for sale:
https://www.zazzle.ca/store/kelly_falardeau

To set up your own merchandise store, go to:
https://www.zazzle.ca/store/kelly_falardeau?rf=238495416043823104

NOTES:

Exercise for Module 8
Crafting Your Online Course

This exercise is designed to help you take the first steps in creating your online course. Buckle up, because we're about to dive into the world of digital academia!

Step 1: The Course Concept

Start by summarizing the concept of your course in one sentence. This is essentially your course's elevator pitch. Think of it as the subtitle for your book's online course edition.

Step 2: The Curriculum Crafter

Based on the content of your book, outline the main modules for your course. Under each module, list the key lessons or topics that you will cover. This is your preliminary curriculum. Remember, your curriculum should flow logically and lead the students toward a clear objective.

Step 3: The Lecture Lab

Choose one lesson from your curriculum and plan out a short lecture. Write down the key points you want to cover, any visual aids or props you would need, and any anecdotes or jokes you could tell. Consider this as a mini-script for your lecture.

Step 4: The Interaction Initiator

Think about how you can engage your students. What questions could you ask them? What tasks could you set for them? How would you encourage them to participate in discussions? Draft a plan for student interaction for the lesson you chose in Step 3.

Step 5: The Selling Script

Finally, draft a promotional blurb for your course that would make your readers (or anyone else) want to sign up. Highlight the benefits of the course, what students will learn, and why you are the perfect teacher for this course.

This exercise should help you kickstart your online course creation process. It will help you outline your course, plan your lectures, and think about how to engage your students. Remember, your course is an extension of your book, so keep the tone, style, and content consistent. Happy planning!

NOTES:

Exercise for Module 9
Becoming a Consultant

This exercise is designed to help you take the first steps into becoming a consultant. It's time to swap your author's pen for a consultant's cap!

Step 1: The Service Suitcase

Start by identifying the key insights, lessons, or skills from your book that could be valuable to others. Jot down these wisdom nuggets - they're what you're packing in your consultancy service suitcase.

Step 2: The Client Carousel

Next, brainstorm potential clients who could benefit from your wisdom. Think about industries, companies, organizations, or individuals that are relevant to your book's subject. Remember, your clients could come from surprising places, so don't limit yourself.

Step 3: The Service Sketch

Now, think about how you could deliver your wisdom. Could you offer one-on-one sessions, workshops, keynote speeches, or advisory roles? Sketch out at least three different services you could offer, based on your wisdom nuggets and potential clients.

Step 4: The Marketing Mindmap

Time to think about how you could market your services. How can you use your book, your network, and your online presence to attract clients? Create a mindmap with your book at the center and different marketing tactics branching out.

Step 5: The Trial Test

Lastly, pick one potential client (it could be a company, organization, or individual) and one service you've sketched out. How would you approach this client? What would you say to convince them of your services' value? Write down a brief pitch that you could use.

This exercise should provide a starting point in your journey toward becoming a consultant. Remember, your book is your foundation, your wisdom is your product, and your personality is your selling point. Happy planning!

NOTES:

Exercise for Module 10
Podcasting - Your Book, Unplugged and Unscripted

This exercise will help you plan your podcasting journey. Get ready to tune into your book's auditory potential!

Step 1: The Podcast Proposal

Start by outlining the concept for your podcast. What will it be about? How is it linked to your book? How many episodes are you planning? Draft a one-paragraph proposal for your podcast, just like you would for a book.

Step 2: The Episode Outline

Next, sketch out an outline for your first episode. What are the key points you want to cover? Are there any stories, anecdotes, or jokes you could include? Who would you interview, if anyone? Plan your episode as if it were a Module in a book.

Step 3: The Technical Tune-Up

Research and list the technical equipment and software you'll need to record your podcast. Remember, good audio quality is crucial for a successful podcast. You don't need to break the bank, but ensure your voice comes through crystal clear.

Step 4: The Promotion Plan

Time to think about marketing your podcast. How will you leverage your existing platforms (book, website, social media) to promote your podcast? Will you use any other promotional methods? Sketch out a preliminary promotion plan.

Step 5: The Fun Factor

Finally, brainstorm ways to inject humor into your podcast. Could you tell funny anecdotes? Use amusing sound effects? Throw in a joke or two? Write down at least five ways you could make your podcast entertaining.

This exercise should help you conceptualize your podcast, plan your first episode, identify the necessary equipment, strategize your promotion, and add a dash of humor. Remember, your podcast should reflect your book's tone and content, so keep it consistent and true to your brand. Happy planning!

Check out: https://hiro.fm?fpr=kelly14 for the best podcasting app.

NOTES:

Exercise for Module 11
The Sequel - Because Your Book Deserves a Franchise

This exercise will help you lay the groundwork for your sequel or prequel. Get ready to extend your literary universe!

Step 1: The Sequel Survey

Start by identifying what your readers loved about your original book. You can do this through reviews, feedback, or even a quick survey. Make a list of the top 5 things your readers enjoyed. These elements will form the foundation of your sequel.

Step 2: The Character Canvas

Choose one character from your original book for whom you'd like to create a backstory or an extended plotline. Sketch a brief outline of this character's journey in the sequel or prequel.

Step 3: The Prequel Preview

If you're thinking of a prequel, outline the backstory or history you want to explore. What key events shaped your characters or their world before the original book's timeline? Draft a short summary of your prequel's plot.

Step 4: The Humor Blueprint

Humor is your secret weapon. Brainstorm some funny scenarios, dialogues, or incidents that could occur in your sequel or prequel. Write down at least five humorous moments that could lighten up your next book.

Step 5: The Title Teaser

Lastly, come up with a working title for your sequel or prequel. Make it catchy and indicative of your book's content or character. Remember, your title is the first thing your readers will see, so make it intriguing!

This exercise should help you visualize your sequel or prequel, understand what your readers want, identify which character or backstory to explore, brainstorm humorous elements, and come up with a working title. So, let your imagination run wild and start building your book franchise. Happy writing!

NOTES:

Exercise for Module 12
Writing Workshops - Become the Yoda for Your Luke Skywalkers

This exercise will guide you in planning your first writing workshop. Buckle up; it's time to teach!

Step 1: The Workshop Whys

Start by outlining why you want to host a writing workshop. What knowledge do you want to share? How can you help aspiring writers? Write a short mission statement for your workshop.

Step 2: The Lesson Layout

Next, plan the structure of your workshop. What topics will you cover? How will you break down the workshop? Will it be a one-off session or a series? Draft a brief agenda or curriculum for your workshop.

Step 3: The Funny Factor

Identify ways to inject humor into your workshop. Could you share amusing anecdotes from your writing journey? Plan funny writing exercises? Incorporate humorous ice breakers? List at least five ways to make your workshop entertaining.

Step 4: The Audience Assessment

Who is your target audience for the workshop? Beginner writers? Advanced authors? A specific genre? Define your target audience and write a brief description of them.

Step 5: The Promotion Plan

Finally, consider how you will promote your workshop. Will you leverage your book? Use social media? Send out a newsletter? Draft a basic promotion plan.

This exercise will help you define the purpose of your workshop, plan your curriculum, identify ways to make it entertaining, understand your target audience, and strategize promotion. This workshop isn't just a monetization method; it's a way to give back to the writing community. So, enjoy the process and happy teaching!

NOTES:

Exercise for Module 13
The Book-to-Screen Bonanza - Hollywood, Here We Come!

This exercise will help you visualize your book as a potential screen adaptation. It's time to roll out the red carpet for your masterpiece!

Step 1: The Script Selection

Choose a scene from your book that you believe would translate well onto the screen. This could be a pivotal moment, a dramatic climax, or a scene with particularly humorous dialogue. Write it down.

Step 2: The Scene Rewrite

Now, rewrite this scene as a screenplay. Remember, screenplays focus more on the visual and audible aspects of a scene. Don't worry about getting it perfect; this is just a fun exercise to visualize your book in a new medium.

Step 3: The Casting Call

Time for some imaginary casting! For each of your main characters, choose an actor or actress you believe would best represent them on screen. Be playful with this; you could even cast comedians as serious characters for a humorous twist!

Step 4: The Hilarity Highlights

Think about how you could inject humor into your scene if it were to be adapted. What comedic moments could be added? How could the dialogue or situation be tweaked for a laugh? Jot down at least three funny elements.

Step 5: The Premiere Visualization

Finally, visualize your book's premiere. Picture the red carpet, the flashing cameras, the buzzing crowd. Who would you invite? What would you wear? Write a brief description of your dream book-to-screen premiere.

This exercise will help you explore the potential of your book for a screen adaptation, play around with the idea of casting, find humor in the visual and audible aspects of a scene, and even dream a little about a Hollywood premiere. Enjoy the process, and remember: in this exercise, the sky's the limit!

NOTES:

Exercise for Module 14
Book Tours - It's Like a Road Trip, but with Books!

This exercise will guide you through the initial planning stages of a hypothetical book tour, with a humorous twist. So grab your map, your sense of adventure, and of course, your book, and let's hit the road!

Step 1: The Destination Dreaming

Start by making a wish-list of destinations for your book tour. Don't limit yourself - if you want to host a book signing in a hot air balloon over Paris, add it to the list!

Step 2: The Venue Vision

Next, for each destination, think of an unusual, funny, or interesting venue where you could host a book event. A haunted house? A retro bowling alley? A serene park where local squirrels can also attend?

Step 3: The Promo Pranks

Think of humorous ways to promote your book tour. Could you create a comic strip? A goofy travel vlog with your book 'visiting' various sites? Or perhaps a faux news report about your book's journey?

Step 4: The Reader Rendezvous

Plan some funny ice-breakers or activities for your audience during the book events. A joke-telling contest? A hilarious reenactment of a scene from your book? Or a "Dress as a Character" competition from your book?

Step 5: The Travel Tales

Finally, write a short, humorous 'travel diary' entry from the perspective of your book. Did it enjoy the view from the top of the Empire State Building? Or maybe it had a close encounter with a seagull at the beach?

This exercise is not only a fun way to explore the concept of a book tour but also encourages you to think creatively about promoting your book and engaging with your readers. So enjoy the journey, and remember - it's not just about the destination, it's about the book-filled adventure along the way!

NOTES:

Exercise for Module 15
Merchandising Your Masterpiece - From T-Shirts to Teapots

In this exercise, we'll embrace the humor and creativity from this Module to design your own line of book-themed merchandise. Don't worry, you won't actually have to produce or sell anything, unless you want to!

Step 1: The Product Brainstorming

Write down a list of 10 potential merchandise items related to your book. They could be as common as t-shirts and mugs or as outrageous as inflatable unicorns branded with your book's title. Yes, really!

Step 2: The Design Doodles

Choose three items from your list and sketch a rough design for each. It's not about artistic talent, but rather about capturing the essence of your book in a humorous way. If your book is a dramatic thriller, perhaps a glow-in-the-dark bookmark with the quote "I couldn't put it down, even in the dark!" would make for an amusing piece.

Step 3: The Tagline Twist

Next, come up with a funny tagline for each of your merchandise items. If you've chosen to design a scarf, for instance, with prints of your book's most romantic quotes, your tagline could be something like, "Stay warm with the heated words of passion from my book!"

Step 4: The Mock Advertisement

Now, write a short, humorous advertisement for one of your merchandise items. Make it as quirky, silly, or over-the-top as you like! This is your chance to really sell the humor and uniqueness of your product.

Step 5: The Feedback Fun

Share your merchandise ideas, designs, taglines, and advertisements with friends or family. See which ones get the biggest laughs or the most interest. Who knows, you might find some real potential for your merchandising!

Remember, this exercise is all about having fun, thinking outside the box, and finding new, unique ways to connect with your readers. So let loose, get creative, and remember: in the world of book merchandising, the sky's the limit!

NOTES:

Exercise for Module 16
Ebooks, Audiobooks and Puppet Shows, Oh My! - The Art of Repurposing Content

In this exercise, let's flex our creative muscles and delve into the fun and surprising ways we can repurpose the content of your book. Remember, humor and creativity are your guiding stars here.

Step 1: The Ebooks Epiphany

Jot down five unique features you could incorporate into an ebook version of your book. This could be interactive images, embedded audio clips, or even a digital treasure hunt within the pages. The wilder, the better!

Step 2: The Audiobooks Adventure

Imagine your book as an audiobook. Who would you want to narrate it? Write a humorous letter to your dream narrator, be it a celebrity, a fictional character, or your high school drama teacher, explaining why you think their voice is perfect for your book.

Step 3: The Puppet Shows Parade

Design a basic puppet show scene from your book. Describe the puppets, the set, and the dialogue. Can you imagine your dignified protagonist as a marionette? The dramatic possibilities are endless!

Step 4: The Comics and Graphic Novels Gala

Sketch a short comic strip or storyboard of a scene from your book. If you're artistically challenged, stick figures are perfectly acceptable! Focus on the funny aspects of your story.

Step 5: The Board Games Bonanza

Outline a simple board game based on your book. What are the rules? How do you win? Are there any ridiculous penalties for landing on certain squares? Let your imagination run wild!

Step 6: The Feedback Fiesta

Share your ideas with friends, family, or fellow writers. Which ones get the biggest laughs or spark the most interest? You might find that your humorous repurposing ideas are not just entertaining, but could also become a reality!

Have fun with this exercise and remember: when it comes to repurposing content, the sky is the limit. Or, as we say in the repurposing business, the book is the beginning!

NOTES:

Repurpose Your Content with Repurpose.io

Imagine if you could...

Take one item of Content...

Transform it into **THIRTY** items of content **in seconds**...

And then distribute all 30 across **ALL** your social media channels...

And have it happen on auto-pilot.

Sound amazing?

Check out this bad boy...

https://repurpose.io/?aff=16788

Exercise for Module 17: "The Dollar Dance - Patreon and Crowdfunding Your Way to Bestseller Status"

This exercise aims to get your creative juices flowing and prepare you to dive into the world of Patreon and crowdfunding. Let's get started with some funny and engaging tasks.

Step 1: The Patreon Proposal

Envision your Patreon page. What tiers would you set? What rewards would you offer? Get creative and humorous with it. For example, at a $50 tier, perhaps you offer to write a short story about the patron's pet. Or, for $100, you could create a dramatic reading of your book's most intense scene, complete with sock puppets!

Step 2: The Crowdfunding Campaign

Plan out a mock crowdfunding campaign for your book. What's your elevator pitch? What rewards would you offer? Maybe at a $250 pledge level, backers get a cameo in your book where they share a comically trivial interaction with the main character.

Step 3: The Perks and Pitfalls Brainstorm

List out potential perks and pitfalls of Patreon and crowdfunding. Then, create funny solutions or workarounds for the pitfalls. Got a pitfall of having to handwrite 200 thank-you notes? Solution: Develop a sudden and specific bout of amnesia that affects only your handwriting ability.

Step 4: The Promotional Video

Outline a script for a promotional video for your crowdfunding campaign. This is your chance to showcase your book and your personality. Make it funny, make it heartfelt, and most importantly, make it you. Remember, a good laugh can turn a maybe into a definite yes!

Step 5: The Feedback Fiesta

Share your ideas with your writing peers, friends, or family. Which ones make them chuckle or pique their interest? Remember, this exercise is all about exploring possibilities and finding humor in the process.

Keep in mind that while Patreon and crowdfunding can be daunting, they are also platforms for you to express your creativity and engage directly with your readers. So, put on your dancing shoes and start practicing the Dollar Dance!

NOTES:

Exercise for Module 18
Rolling in the Dough - Unleashing the Power of Sponsored Content"

This exercise aims to help you explore the concept of sponsored content in a fun, light-hearted way. So, let's hop on board the sponsored content train - next stop, Funnyville!

Step 1: The Product Hunt

First, make a list of products or brands that could fit naturally (or hilariously unnaturally) into your book. Remember, it doesn't have to be perfect - it could be as outlandish as an apocalypse survivor with a penchant for designer shoes or a medieval knight who swears by his branded chainmail cleaner.

Step 2: The Pitch Party

Choose your top three products or brands from your list. Now, write a brief pitch for each, explaining why and how they would be a good fit for your book. Don't shy away from humor here - the more outrageous, the better!

Step 3: The Sneaky Placement

Pick one product from the list and write a short scene where your character interacts with the product in a funny or surprising way. Remember, the aim is to make your readers laugh, not to give them a hard sell.

Step 4: The Reality Check

Now, think about how your readers would react to this scene. Would they find it funny, or would they roll their eyes at the obvious product placement? Write a paragraph or two about how you could tweak the scene to make it more humorous and less sales-y.

Step 5: The Feedback Frenzy

Finally, share your scene and your pitches with a friend or a writing group. Which ones do they find the most amusing? Would they be annoyed or entertained by the product placement?

Remember, the key to successful (and funny) sponsored content is creativity. Don't be afraid to think outside the box, and above all, don't forget to have fun! After all, if you can't have a good laugh at a knight polishing his chainmail with a branded cleaner, then what's the point of it all?

NOTES:

Exercise for Module 19
Join the Club - The Art of Building a (Not So) Secret Society via a Membership Site"

This exercise will let your creative juices flow and help you visualize your potential membership site in a fun and engaging way. Think of it as your private clubhouse, where only the funniest and most book-obsessed folks are allowed. Ready? Here we go!

Step 1: The Concept Comedy

First things first, jot down what the concept of your membership site would be. Remember to keep it related to your book or writing. Maybe it's a digital speakeasy for fans of humorous literature or a secret society for folks who love to laugh while reading. Keep it light, keep it fun!

Step 2: The Freemium Fable

Next, decide if you'd want to have a freemium model. Write a short, comical story explaining why a member upgraded from the free tier. Did they fall in love with your daily 'Joke of the Day' post? Were they enticed by the promise of monthly personalized limericks?

Step 3: Content Carnival

List down five types of content you'd like to share with your members. Make each one as quirky as possible! Will there be a 'Monday Meme Madness' or 'Friday Night Fiction Fights' where members debate about plot points in your book? The sillier, the better!

Step 4: The Community Charade

Visualize the kind of community you want to build. Will your members help each other to write funnier, better, faster? Or will there be an annual 'Silly Sentence Championship'? Write a brief dialogue between two members interacting on your site.

Step 5: The Pitfall Parade

Lastly, identify potential pitfalls and challenges with your membership site and, more importantly, comical solutions to them. For instance, what if a member is spamming others with puns? Maybe the solution is a 'Pun Jail' where they are sentenced to a week of only serious discussions!

Remember, the goal here is not just to plan, but to have fun while doing it. This exercise should get you laughing, brainstorming, and a step closer to having your very own online club.

NOTES:

Exercise for Module 20
Ads-olutely Hilarious - The World of Advertising Revenue

This exercise will help you think about advertising opportunities in a light-hearted and playful way.

Step 1: The Ad Lib Game

List down three products or services that are relevant to the theme of your book. Now, write a short, humorous ad for each one in your author's voice. These should be ads that your readers might find amusing and relevant enough not to skip.

Step 2: Pick a Partner

Think about three businesses or brands that align well with your book's content. Imagine you're pitching an ad space to them. Write a funny pitch for each brand, explaining why your book is the perfect place for their advertisement.

Step 3: Affiliate Amusement

Consider an item or service that features prominently in your book, one that you can promote via affiliate marketing. Create a funny promo blurb that you could add to your book or website, enticing readers to purchase the item or service.

Step 4: Content, Sponsored by...

Consider a potential scenario where a brand wants to sponsor content in your book. How would you integrate their product into your story without disrupting the narrative? Write a short, humorous scenario incorporating the product.

Step 5: Network Noodling

Research some online ad networks and imagine you're explaining what they do to a five-year-old, using humorous and simplified terms. This can help you understand their functions and perhaps even find a funny way to explain them to your readers.

This exercise should help you get into the right mindset to explore advertising revenue in a fun and humorous way, allowing you to benefit from it without sacrificing reader engagement.

NOTES:

Exercise for Module 23
Leveraging Social Media - The Comedy Cruise

Hop aboard the comedy cruise ship, my friends! We're about to take a joyride through the fun and fabulous world of social media. Get ready for some engagement, entertainment, and maybe even a few 'e-laughs'. Buckle up!

Step 1: Your Humor Hashtag

Create a funny hashtag related to your book or your writing journey. The quirkier, the better! Maybe it's #AdventuresInTypos or #LateNightWriterWoes. Remember, make it something unique that your readers can latch onto and share.

Step 2: Instagrammable Moments

Take a picture of your writing space or your favorite writing snack. Now, caption it with something funny. It could be a witty observation or a pun. Post it on Instagram with your newly created hashtag.

Step 3: Tweet a Joke

Time to flex those comedy muscles! Tweet a joke or a funny observation about your writing process, and don't forget to use your unique hashtag.

Step 4: Facebook Fun

Create a funny meme related to your book's genre or topic and post it on your Facebook page. Encourage your followers to share it and use your hashtag.

Step 5: TikTok Challenge

This one is for the brave! Create a funny TikTok video related to your book. It could be a hilarious book trailer, a 'day in the life' video, or even a funny skit. Use your hashtag and challenge your followers to duet with you.

Step 6: LinkedIn Laughs

Post a light-hearted article on LinkedIn about the highs and lows of the writing process. Inject it with humor and relatability to connect with your professional network.

Remember, these exercises aren't just tasks to check off a list; they're opportunities to engage with your readers and make them smile. Happy sailing in the ocean of social media!

NOTES:

Exercise for Module 24
Donations and Tip Jars - The Writer's Gold Rush

Let's embark on a gold-digging adventure, fellow prospectors, but don't worry, we're not looking for actual gold (unless your readers are particularly generous). This exercise is about setting up your own virtual tip jar and making it an appealing, welcoming spot for your readers to drop in their support. Ready? Let's go!

Step 1: Choose Your Platform

Decide on the platform you will use for your virtual tip jar. It could be PayPal, Ko-fi, Patreon, or any other digital payment platform. Don't fret over choosing the 'best' one. Just pick the one that resonates most with you and is easy for your readers to use.

Step 2: Write Your Pitch

Create a friendly, light-hearted message asking for donations. Remember, it's not begging; it's inviting your readers to support your craft. Let's try something like, "Enjoying the ride? Help fuel my writing journey with a cup of coffee (or two)!". You get the drift.

Step 3: Place Your Pitch

Choose the best spots to place your message. It could be your author bio, at the end of your chapters, or on your website. Visibility is key here. Your donation button should be like a neon sign at a roadside diner - impossible to miss!

Step 4: Say Thank You

Draft a warm, sincere thank you message for those who donate. It can be humorous too, like, "You just made my coffee machine the happiest appliance in the house. Thanks a latte!" A little gratitude can go a long way.

Step 5: Promote Your Tip Jar

Share your donation link on your social media platforms. This can be a simple, funny post like, "Join my support squad and ensure I never write hangry. Donate here to keep me caffeinated!"

Step 6: Review & Revise

After a week or two, review your results. Is your tip jar visible enough? Is your pitch enticing? Could your thank you message be warmer? If needed, tweak your approach, and repeat steps 2 to 5 until you strike gold!

NOTES:

Exercise for Module 25
Becoming a Freelance Ghostwriter - The Literary Batman

Step 1: Batcave Exploration

First, identify your genre preferences. Are you a comic book wizard, a romance aficionado, a thriller enthusiast, or a sci-fi fanatic? List down your favorite genres and why you like them. This will help you determine the kinds of projects you'll most enjoy as a ghostwriter or freelancer.

Step 2: Batman's Utility Belt

Analyze your writing strengths. Are you great at creating engaging characters? Is your forte in crafting riveting dialogue? Do your plot twists leave readers in awe? Like Batman's Utility Belt, these are your tools. List them down.

Step 3: Bat-Signal Creation

Create a sample piece of writing in your preferred genre showcasing your strengths from step 2. This will serve as your Bat-Signal, calling out to potential clients.

Step 4: Batmobile Test Drive

Take a freelance or ghostwriting job for a spin! Look for a small, short-term project on platforms like Upwork or Fiverr to start with. It could be as simple as writing a blog post or a short story. It's like your first drive in the Batmobile.

Step 5: Meeting Commissioner Gordon

After completing your first project, seek feedback. This is like meeting Commissioner Gordon - gaining insights and intelligence on how you can improve. Take note of what went well and what challenges you faced.

Step 6: Alfred's Words of Wisdom

Reflect on your experience. Did you enjoy the anonymity of ghostwriting? Did you love the variety of freelancing? Remember, like Alfred was for Batman, self-reflection is an essential guide for your journey.

Step 7: Embracing Your Batman

Based on your reflection, make a decision. Are you ready to fully embrace the life of a freelance ghostwriter, or do you need to prepare more? Either way, remember, every Batman starts somewhere! Keep honing your craft and take on new projects as you grow comfortable.

Don't forget to laugh and have fun on this journey. After all, even Batman cracks a smile once in a while!

NOTES:

Exercise for Module 26
The Great Book Leveraging Challenge

Alright, it's time to roll up those sleeves and get those creative juices flowing! Here's a fun (and slightly goofy) exercise to help you start thinking about how you can leverage your book. Don't worry, no beavers were harmed in the making of this exercise.

Step 1: The Egg Transformation

Take a key point or idea from your book. Now, pretend this idea is an egg. How many ways can you cook this egg? In other words, how many different forms can this idea take? Write down at least five, whether it's a blog post, podcast episode, social media post, infographic, or even a song!

Step 2: Sequel Mania

If your book were a movie, what would the sequel look like? Write a short blurb for a potential follow-up. Remember, it should deepen the conversation, not just rehash what's already been said.

Step 3: The Collaboration Invitation

Think of another author whose work complements yours. How could you collaborate? Maybe a joint webinar or a combined special edition? Sketch out a rough idea of what this collaboration might look like.

Step 4: The Global Book Tour

Imagine your book in three different languages. Which languages would you choose? How could your book's content benefit readers in those language-speaking countries? Write a short pitch for each.

Step 5: The Beaver's Perspective

Now, think like a beaver. Yep, you heard me right. What opportunities are there for you to build and expand upon what you already have? Remember, the beaver is all about resourcefulness and hard work. Make a list of at least three opportunities.

NOTES:

Exercise for Module 27
Embracing Your Inner YouTube Star

Part 1: Find Your Niche

Start by finding a topic for your YouTube channel. It should align with the subject of your book to create a cohesive brand. Ask yourself, "What value can I provide to my viewers?" Is it expert knowledge, motivation, humor, a behind-the-scenes look at your author journey?

Part 2: Practice Talking to the Camera

Practice makes perfect, and the first step towards becoming comfortable on camera is to start practicing. Grab your phone or a camera and start recording yourself talking. It might feel awkward at first (it will, trust me), but the more you do it, the more natural it will feel. Practice speaking clearly and confidently about your book's topic.

Part 3: Plan Your First Video

What would your first video be about? Write an outline or a script, but remember to keep it conversational. Include a brief introduction about yourself and why you are an expert in the field. Discuss the main points you want to cover in your video and conclude with a call-to-action, encouraging viewers to like, subscribe, and check out your book.

Part 4: Create Your YouTube Account

Go ahead, take the plunge and set up your YouTube channel. Use a professional picture for your profile, preferably one of you smiling - remember, you're going to be someone's new virtual best friend!

Part 5: Record, Edit, Upload

Time to put your plan into action. Record your first video, and remember, it doesn't have to be perfect. Be genuine and offer value. After recording, edit your video to make it more engaging. Once you're satisfied, upload your masterpiece to your channel.

Bonus Part: Engage With Your Viewers

Once your video is live, remember to engage with your viewers. Answer their comments, thank them for their views, and be active in your own channel. It'll help build a community around your content.

NOTES:

Exercise for Module 28
Writing Sequels

1. The "Previously on..." Summary: Just like your favorite TV shows do a "Previously on...", do the same for your book. Write a one-page summary of your last book focusing on key plot points, characters, and unresolved threads that will transition into your sequel. Ensure you are capturing the core essence of your story and any cliffhangers that would lead your reader to the next book.

2. The Character Evolution Matrix: On a piece of paper, write down the names of your main characters. Next to each name, jot down the emotional, physical, and intellectual state of the character at the end of the last book. Then write where you want them to be by the end of the sequel. This exercise will help you understand the journey each character needs to take in your sequel.

3. Plot Twist Generator: Write down ten potential plot twists for your sequel. The wilder, the better. Now pick your favorite three. Try to incorporate at least one of these into your sequel.

4. Subtitle Synthesis: Sequels often have subtitles to differentiate them from the first book, but also to hint at the new plot or theme. Spend some time brainstorming ten possible subtitles for your sequel. This will help you to further solidify the unique elements of your next book.

5. Pineapple Problem: Just for fun, create a ridiculous plot inconsistency (like a character being allergic to pineapples in the first book but not in the sequel). Now, come up with a creative explanation to resolve this inconsistency. This exercise will get your creative juices flowing and prepare you for managing potential plot inconsistencies in your sequel.

Remember, sequels are meant to continue the story, but they should also have their own unique narrative and charm. So buckle up and get ready for the wild ride!

NOTES:

Exercise for Module 29
Comparable Services, or the Art of Not Selling the Brooklyn Bridge

1. The Brainstorm Brew: Grab a steaming cup of your favorite brew (coffee, tea, or a cold brewski, no judgment here!) and let's get the brain juices flowing. Make a list of all possible services or products related to your book's content. Let the ideas flow - no matter how wacky they are! Remember, we're just brainstorming here, even the Brooklyn Bridge seemed like a silly idea at first!

2. Rate the Great: Now that you have a list that might rival the size of your laundry pile, let's sift through it. Rate each idea on a scale of 1-10 based on its feasibility and relevance to your book.

3. Pitch Perfect: Pick your top three ideas from the previous step. Now, imagine you're in an elevator with a potential reader or a shark from Shark Tank, and you have 30 seconds to sell your idea to them. Write down these pitches and remember, make them as compelling as a finale episode cliffhanger!

4. Test Run: Got your pitches? Great! Now, find a friendly guinea pig (metaphorical, not literal) - a friend, family member, or a social media follower, and pitch your ideas. Gather their feedback and notice their reactions.

5. Refine and Shine: Take the feedback you received and refine your ideas. Hone your pitches, tweak the services, add some more glitter or remove the unicorns if needed. Repeat this process until you have a set of comparable services you are confident to sell, preferably without including any monumental bridges.

NOTES:

Exercise for Module 30
Leveraging Email Marketing

Step 1: Identify Your Readers' Interests

Identify three interests or needs of your readers that are related to your book. Think about what made them pick up your book in the first place and what they might want to learn more about.

For example, if you wrote a book on knitting dog sweaters, your readers might be interested in learning more advanced knitting techniques, discovering the best materials for pet-friendly clothes, or even understanding how to start a pet clothing business.

Step 2: Create Your Call to Action

Based on these interests, draft a call to action (CTA) to entice readers to join your email list. Make sure your CTA communicates clearly what the reader can expect to gain by signing up. Remember to add some humor!

Step 3: Plan Your Email Content

Think about the type of content that would provide value to your readers while aligning with your book's topic. It could be tips, exclusive content, related product recommendations, or updates about your work. Plan the first three emails you would send to your subscribers.

Step 4: Research Affiliate Programs

Find three products or services that would benefit your audience and have affiliate programs that you could join. These will be the products or services you could recommend to your email list in the future.

Step 5: Practice Writing an Email

Now, write a draft email to your potential subscribers introducing one of the products you've identified in step 4. Remember to include why you're recommending it, how it can benefit the reader, and a call to action prompting them to check it out. Don't forget to sprinkle some humor in your email!

By the end of this exercise, you'll have a better understanding of how to start your email marketing strategy and provide value to your readers while also monetizing your emails in a fun and engaging way.

NOTES:

Exercise for Module 31
Design Your First Live Event

For this exercise, let's dive into the world of event planning! But remember, we're not just planning any event; we're designing an unforgettable experience for your fans that also drives revenue. So let's get started!

Step 1: Identify your event's purpose and theme

First things first: What's the point of your event? Are you promoting your book, celebrating a launch, diving deep into your book's themes, or something else? Write down the purpose of your event.

Next, brainstorm potential themes that align with your book's content and your event's purpose. Your theme can be as literal or symbolic as you want, so have fun with it! Write down at least three different theme ideas.

Step 2: Sketch your ideal venue

Now, think about where you'd like to host your event. Consider factors such as location, size, and ambiance. Sketch or describe your ideal venue and explain why it suits your event's theme and purpose.

Step 3: Plan your event's main attraction

Every good event has a star attraction. What's yours going to be? A dramatic reading? A panel discussion with other authors? A book signing? Remember to make it something that your attendees would be willing to pay for. Write down your main attraction, and think about how it aligns with your theme and purpose.

Step 4: Plan your promotional strategy

Finally, think about how you'll get people to come to your event. Will you send out an exclusive invite to your mailing list? Tease it on social media? Partner with local businesses for cross-promotion? Write down at least three promotional strategies.

Remember, this exercise is just the beginning. Event planning involves a lot of details and coordination, but with careful planning, you can create an unforgettable, monetized experience for your fans!

NOTES:

SHOW ME THE MONEY!

Roll up your sleeves and fasten your seatbelts folks, we're about to embark on the roller coaster ride known as "Show Me the Money!" In this thrill-a-minute adventure, we'll explore how your literary masterpieces can morph into your own personal money printing machine, thanks to a little thing we call cash flow projections.

A cash flow projection, or as we like to call it, the "Ka-Ching Forecast", is a super useful tool to estimate how much moolah you could be raking in from your book. We're not talking about just selling your book here; no, no, we're looking at an entire cornucopia of potential earnings.

First up, we have the good ol' book sales. It's like selling lemonade on a hot day, but instead of a cool refreshing drink, it's your literary genius in print form. Next on the agenda is an Audiobook, where you'll be serenading your audience with your silky smooth voice.

Then we have speaking gigs. Who wouldn't pay to hear you, the literary savant, share wisdom and anecdotes? If you fancy being the star of your show, hosting live events or even coaching and consulting, can pack a powerful financial punch.

We also venture into the digital realm with online courses, Patreon memberships, and merchandise. And hey, let's not forget the traditional method of sponsorships.

Each of these methods has the potential to fill your pockets, but how much exactly? Well, sit tight because we're about to find out!

Monthly Memberships

Monthly memberships? Think of it like a hot nightclub and you're the dazzling DJ, dropping the beats (or in this case, books). Your fans are lining up behind that velvet rope, willing to pay a cover charge just to get close to the action. Except, in this glittering literary disco, they're signing up for a monthly fee to get VIP access to your word wizardry. With every new dance partner, your monthly income does the cha-ching cha-cha! It's the dance-off that pays off, so it's time to turn on the disco ball and get the party started!

SCENARIO: Here is a 12-month projection based selling a $50 per month membership:

MONTH	REVENUE (SALES)	COSTS	NET CASH FLOW
1	$1000 ($50 membership * 20 members)	$500 (website setup, marketing)	$500
2	$1500 ($50 membership * 30 members)	$300 (site maintenance, marketing)	$1200
3	$2000 ($50 membership * 40 members)	$300 (site maintenance, marketing)	$1700
4	$2500 ($50 membership * 50 members)	$300 (site maintenance, marketing)	$2200
5	$3000 ($50 membership * 60 members)	$300 (site maintenance, marketing)	$2700
6	$3500 ($50 membership * 70 members)	$300 (site maintenance, marketing)	$3200
7	$4000 ($50 membership * 80 members)	$300 (site maintenance, marketing)	$3700
8	$4500 ($50 membership * 90 members)	$300 (site maintenance, marketing)	$4200
9	$5000 ($50 membership * 100 members)	$300 (site maintenance, marketing)	$4700
10	$5000 ($50 membership * 100 members)	$300 (site maintenance, marketing)	$4700
11	$5000 ($50 membership * 100 members)	$300 (site maintenance, marketing)	$4700

12	$5000 ($50 membership * 100 members)	$300 (site maintenance, marketing)	$4700
TOTAL	**$42,000 + 840 MEMBERS (WHO YOU CAN SELL OTHER PRODUCTS & SERVICES TO)**	**$3800**	**$38,200**

The revenue is calculated as the monthly membership fee multiplied by the number of members. The costs here are simplified, representing website maintenance and marketing costs.

POTENTIAL REVENUE FOR 840 MEMBERS PAYING YOU $50 PER MONTH IS $38,200 PER YEAR IN YEAR ONE.

Let's project you don't have any more growth and you consistently have 840 members paying you $50 per month - you would make $42,000 per month or $504,000 per year. That's half a million dollars in one year. Wowsa!

Remember, these numbers are purely hypothetical. Your costs might include other elements like the cost of creating content, hiring staff, taxes, transaction charges, etc. Also, your revenue might grow at a different pace.

SELLING AUDIO BOOKS

Ah, audiobooks. What's not to love? You get to whisper sweet nothings (or suspenseful somethings) into your reader's ear from the comfort of their car, their home, or heck, even their bathroom.

It's like you're there, but without any of the awkward eye contact. You could be reading your book in your PJs while they're stuck in traffic, and they'll be thanking you for it! With every "read," your bank account gets a sound boost.

So, roll out of bed and into the recording studio, it's time to give your book the voice it deserves!

CHECK OUT HIRO.FM FOR MY FAVE AUDIO PLATFORM TO HOST YOUR BOOK: https://hiro.fm?fpr=kelly59

Here's a simple cash flow projection for selling an audiobook at a price of $35:

Month	Audiobook Sales Quantity	Price Per Audiobook	Gross Revenue	Production Cost (20%)	Net Revenue
January	100	$35	$3500	$700	$2800
February	110	$35	$3850	$770	$3080
March	120	$35	$4200	$840	$3360
April	130	$35	$4550	$910	$3640
May	140	$35	$4900	$980	$3920
June	150	$35	$5250	$1050	$4200
July	160	$35	$5600	$1120	$4480
August	170	$35	$5950	$1190	$4760
September	180	$35	$6300	$1260	$5040
October	190	$35	$6650	$1330	$5320
November	200	$35	$7000	$1400	$5600
December	210	$35	$7350	$1470	$5880
Total	**1920**		**$67,200**	**$13,440**	**$53,760**

This table is a projection based on a steady growth of 10 additional sales per month and an assumed production cost of 20% of the gross revenue. The net revenue is simply the gross revenue minus the production cost. Note that this is a simple estimate and your actual results may vary depending on various factors such as marketing effectiveness, market demand, and competition.

Based on selling 1920 audiobooks over a 12-month period, you have the potential to make **$53,760.**

SPEAKING GIGS

Speaking gigs, are the equivalent of "stand-up comedy" for authors. Except, you're not exactly throwing out punchlines, but impactful insights, deep thoughts, and stirring anecdotes.

You walk onto the stage, your heart pounding like a drum solo at a rock concert, ready to impart your wisdom, one $3,500 monologue at a time. Don't worry if you're not a natural public speaker; you can always bring a cardboard cutout of yourself for moral support.

The good news? No rotten tomatoes will be thrown your way, just a flood of interested leads and potential book buyers. Time to work on those vocal exercises and shine in the spotlight!

Here's a fantastic way to land more speaking gigs - it's co-founded by my amazing friend Kimberly Crowe - Speakers Playhouse https://kellyfalardeau--checkingout.thrivecart.com/speakersplayhouse/

SCENARIO 1 - SPEAKER FEE $3500 PER GIG - 1 PER MONTH FOR 12 MONTHS

Here's a cash flow projection for conducting speaking gigs at $3500 each for one year, with no increase in gigs or price over time:

Month	No. of Gigs	Price per Gig	Gross Revenue
January	1	$3500	$3500
February	1	$3500	$3500
March	1	$3500	$3500
April	1	$3500	$3500
May	1	$3500	$3500
June	1	$3500	$3500
July	1	$3500	$3500
August	1	$3500	$3500
September	1	$3500	$3500
October	1	$3500	$3500
November	1	$3500	$3500
December	1	$3500	$3500
Total	**12**		**$42,000**

That table assumes a consistent one speaking gig per month for the entire year at a flat rate of $3500 per gig. Please remember that this is a simple estimation and actual results could vary based on numerous factors.

SCENARIO 2: Let's say you earn $3500 per gig PLUS you sell 10% of the room your coaching program for $497

Month	No. of Gigs	Price per Gig	Gross Revenue from Gigs	Attendees Sold to (10%)	Revenue from Coaching
January	1	$3500	$3500	10	$4,970
February	1	$3500	$3500	10	$4,970
March	1	$3500	$3500	10	$4,970
April	1	$3500	$3500	10	$4,970
May $	1	$3500	$3500	10	$4,970
June	1	$3500	$3500	10	$4,970
July	1	$3500	$3500	10	$4,970
August	1	$3500	$3500	10	$4,970
September	1	$3500	$3500	10	$4,970
October	1	$3500	$3500	10	$4,970
November	1	$3500	$3500	10	$4,970
December	1	$3500	$3500	10	$4,970
Total	**12**		**$42,000**	**120**	**$59,640**

So, with a coaching program priced at $497, you'd make a total of $59,640 from the coaching and $42,000 from the speaking gigs, yielding a total annual revenue of $101,640.

As with any financial projection, please remember that these are only estimations and your actual results may vary.

SCENARIO 3: Let's assume the room size is 100 people, and you are selling a $2000 coaching program to 10% of attendees. Here is your cash flow projection for speaking gigs along with the coaching program:

Month	No. of Gigs	Price per Gig	Gross Revenue from Gigs	Attendees Sold to (10%)	Revenue from Coaching
January	1	$3500	$3500	10	$20,000
February	1	$3500	$3500	10	$20,000
March	1	$3500	$3500	10	$20,000
April	1	$3500	$3500	10	$20,000
May	1	$3500	$3500	10	$20,000
June	1	$3500	$3500	10	$20,000
July	1	$3500	$3500	10	$20,000
August	1	$3500	$3500	10	$20,000
September	1	$3500	$3500	10	$20,000
October	1	$3500	$3500	10	$20,000
November	1	$3500	$3500	10	$20,000
December	1	$3500	$3500	10	$20,000
Total	**12**		**$42000**	**120**	**$240,000**

The total annual revenue from the gigs is $42,000, and the coaching program generates an additional $240,000, making a grand total of $282,000 in revenue for the year. As before, please note that these are estimations and actual results can vary.

SCENARIO 4 – SPEAKER FEE $3500 PER GIG – WITH AN INCREASE OF ONE ADDITIONAL GIG EACH MONTH UP TO 6 GIGS PER MONTH

Month	No. of Gigs	Price per Gig	Gross Revenue
January	1	$3500	$350
February	2	$3500	$7000
March	3	$3500	$10500
April	4	$3500	$14000
May	5	$3500	$17500
June	6	$3500	$21000
July	6	$3500	$21000
August	6	$3500	$21000
September	6	$3500	$21000
October	6	$3500	$21000
November	6	$3500	$21000
December	6	$3500	$21000
Total	**61**		**$213,500**

This table assumes a steady growth of one additional gig per month until reaching 6 gigs per month, which then remains consistent for the rest of the year. As always, remember that this is an estimation and actual results could vary.

Now let's make this even more fun. Let's say on month 6 you decide to raise your fee an additional $2000 per gig. Let's do the math on that...

SCENARIO 5: Here's a revised cash flow projection for conducting speaking gigs, with an increase of one additional gig each month up to 6 gigs per month and a fee increase of $2000 per gig from month 6 onward.

Month	No. of Gigs	Price per Gig	Gross Revenue
January	1	$3500	$3500
February	2	$3500	$7000
March	3	$3500	$10500
April	4	$3500	$14000
May	5	$3500	$17500
June	6	$5500	$33000
July	6	$5500	$33000
August	6	$5500	$33000
September	6	$5500	$33000
October	6	$5500	$33000
November	6	$5500	$33000
December	6	$5500	$33000
Total	**61**		**$274,500**

SCENARIO 6: In month 3 they become better in sales and they start selling 20% of the room and then by month 6 they sell 30% of the room for the following months. 100 people paying $50 per ticket to attend the event. Coaching package is $2000.

Here are the projections based on those changes in sales:

Month	Revenue from Ticket Sales	Revenue from Coaching Packages (10% of room for months 1-2, 20% for months 3-5, 30% from month 6 onwards)	Total Revenue
1	$5000	$20,000	$25,000
2	$5000	$20,000	$25,000
3	$5000	$40,000	$45,000

4	$5000	$40,000	$45,000
5	$5000	$40,000	$45,000
6	$5000	$60,000	$65,000
7	$5000	$60,000	$65,000
8	$5000	$60,000	$65,000
9	$5000	$60,000	$65,000
10	$5000	$60,000	$65,000
11	$5000	$60,000	$65,000
12	$5000	$60,000	$65,000
Total Combined Cash Flow Over the Year	$60,000	$580,000	$640,000

Total Cash Flow Over the Year from Coaching Packages (with increasing sales conversion):

Months 1-2 (10% of room): $40,000

Months 3-5 (20% of room): $120,000

Months 6-12 (30% of room): $420,000

Total Combined Cash Flow Over the Year$640,000

Again, this is a simplified projection and doesn't consider expenses or changes in attendance. Sales improvements also often require investment, whether it's through improved marketing, sales training, or other methods.

Let's recap the different scenarios.

Scenario		Potential Revenue
Scenario 1	SPEAKER FEE $3500 PER GIG - 1 PER MONTH FOR 12 MONTHS	$42,000
Scenario 2	$3500 per gig PLUS you sell 10% of the room your coaching program for $497	$59,640
Scenario 3	Room size is 100 people, and you are selling a $2000 coaching program to 10% of attendees	$240,000
Scenario 4	SPEAKER FEE $3500 PER GIG - WITH AN INCREASE OF ONE ADDITIONAL GIG EACH MONTH UP TO 6 GIGS PER MONTH	$213,500
Scenario 5	Up to 6 gigs per month @$3500 and a fee increase of $2000 per gig from month 6 onward:	$274,500
Scenario 6	In month 3 you sell 20% of the room and by month 6 you sell 30% of the room for the following months. 100 people paying $50 per ticket to attend the event. Coaching package is $2000	$640,000

As you can see, it is very easy to generate income from speaking gigs. So get out there and start lining up speaking gigs so you can get your message out there and make a bigger impact and income.

SPONSORSHIPS

Sponsorships are like the fairy godparents of the book world. One moment you're sitting there with a pumpkin and some mice, the next you've got a golden carriage! Ok, maybe it's not exactly like that.

More like you're sitting there with your manuscript, and next thing you know, you're endorsing luxury pens or artisanal coffee that 'stimulates creativity'. Now, just be careful to select the right sponsor.

You wouldn't want to promote edible bookmarks if your readers end up in the ER with paper cuts on their tongues. Let's keep it fun, lucrative, and emergency-room-visit-free, alright?

SCENARIO: For sponsorships, let's say the author secures one sponsorship per month, with each sponsor paying $500 per month for a mention in the book or associated materials (like a podcast or YouTube channel). This projection does not account for taxes or other potential costs.

Month	Number of Sponsorships	Revenue
1	1	$500
2	1	$500
3	1	$500
4	1	$500
5	1	$500
6	1	$500
7	1	$500
8	1	$500
9	1	$500
10	1	$500
11	1	$500
12	1	$500
Total Cash Flow Over the Year		**$6000**

In this scenario, if the author secures sponsorship for $500 per month for a year, they could have a total cash flow of $6000. Please note that this is a simplified projection and actual results can vary based on several factors including negotiation with sponsors and potential costs related to fulfilling sponsorship commitments.

COACHING OR CONSULTING

So, you've written a book. You've climbed the intellectual Everest, and now people want to know how you did it. How did you survive the avalanches of writer's block, the frostbite of self-doubt? Time for some coaching and consulting, my friend!

For a small fee (or a large one, we don't judge), you can become the sherpa guiding aspiring writers up the perilous paths of publishing. Just remember, if your clients ask you about dealing with rejection letters, it's probably best not to suggest 'a good cry and a tub of ice cream' as your first response. Keep it professional, comical, and remember, no one has to know you're doing this in your PJs!

SCENARIO: For coaching or consulting, let's consider a scenario where the author charges $150 per hour. If they take on two clients per week, each with a 2-hour session, the projection would look something like this:

Month	Number of Hours	Revenue
1	16	$2400
2	16	$2400
3	16	$2400
4	16	$2400
5	16	$2400
6	16	$2400
7	16	$2400
8	16	$2400
9	16	$2400
10	16	$2400
11	16	$2400
12	16	$2400
Total Cash Flow Over the Year		**$28,800**

This projection assumes the author consistently has clients and doesn't take time off. Realistically, it might be less if there are gaps between clients or if the author takes time off for vacations, sick leave, etc. Also, remember that this projection does not include any taxes, fees, or costs associated with running the consulting or coaching business.

LIVE EVENTS

Live events - you've read about them, you've seen them in movies, but have you ever actually hosted one? As an author, live events are your chance to be a rock star without having to learn the guitar or, you know, how to sing.

All you have to do is walk out on stage, blinded by spotlight, gripping your book as your only defense against a crowd of readers eager to hear your pearls of wisdom. Easy, right? But wait, there's more!

You also get to see the real-world reactions of your audience as they gasp, laugh, or even fall asleep (hopefully not). So, slap on your best smile, make sure you're wearing pants, and step into the limelight - or at least a well-lit library.

You're not just an author now, you're a performer! Don't worry, it's less like walking a tightrope and more like a fun, slightly nerve-wracking hopscotch.

So let's do some cash flow projections on how much money you can make with live events.

Here's a couple of scenarios...

SCENARIO: Let's consider a scenario where the author charges $50 per ticket for a live event and hosts one event per month, with an average of 100 attendees.

Month	Number of Events	Revenue
1	1	$5000
2	1	$5000
3	1	$5000
4	1	$5000
5	1	$5000
6	1	$5000
7	1	$5000
8	1	$5000
9	1	$5000
10	1	$5000
11	1	$5000
12	1	$5000
Total Cash Flow Over the Year		**$60,000**

This is a simplified projection that assumes the author will consistently be able to sell 100 tickets every month, and it does not take into account any of the expenses associated with organizing a live event. These expenses could include venue rental, equipment, promotion, travel, and more, and they could significantly reduce the net profit from each event.

SCENARIO: Let's make this super conservative. We organize 6 events per year and we add 10% of our revenue is our expenses. 100 people @ $50 per ticket plus selling your $2000 package to 10% of the room.

Month	Event	Revenue from Tickets	Revenue from Coaching Packages (10% of room)	Total Revenue	Expenses (10% of Revenue)	Net Revenue
1	Yes	$5000	$20,000	$25000	$2500	$22500
2	No	$0	$0	$0	$0	$0
3	Yes	$5000	$20,000	$25000	$2500	$22500
4	No	$0	$0	$0	$0	$0
5	Yes	$5000	$20,000	$25000	$2500	$22500
6	No	$0	$0	$0	$0	$0
7	Yes	$5000	$20,000	$25000	$2500	$22500
8	No	$0	$0	$0	$0	$0
9	Yes	$5000	$20,000	$25000	$2500	$22500
10	No	$0	$0	$0	$0	$0
11	Yes	$5000	$20,000	$25000	$2500	$22500
12	No	$0	$0	$0	$0	$0
TOTAL		**$30,000**	**$120,000**	**$150,000**	**$15,000**	**$135,000**

This scenario is more conservative and assumes that you host one event every two months. This allows for more time to plan and market each event, potentially increasing the likelihood of selling tickets and coaching packages. It also factors in expenses which is crucial for a more realistic projection.

SELLING MERCHANDISE

Selling merchandise - it's like having a yard sale, but instead of getting rid of that ceramic cat collection, you're selling stuff people actually want. Items adorned with your book's title or an impactful quote from it, items that even Marie Kondo wouldn't dare suggest you to dispose of.

From T-shirts to coffee mugs, from baseball caps to those hipster tote bags, the possibilities are as endless as the queue at a Black Friday sale. And let's not forget, nothing screams "I am a serious author" more than seeing someone in the street sporting a beanie with your book's title emblazoned across it.

Not to mention, the profit margins are wider than the smile on your face when you receive your first bulk order. Just imagine all your readers, now walking billboards, advertising your book at no extra cost to you. It's like getting your cake, eating it, and then finding out the cake is also a prolific salesperson!

SCENARIO: Assuming the merchandise being sold is t-shirts at $20 each:

Month	Number of T-shirts Sold	Revenue
1	50	$1000
2	60	$1200
3	70	$1400
4	80	$1600
5	90	$1800
6	100	$2000
7	110	$2200
8	120	$2400
9	130	$2600
10	140	$2800
11	150	$3000
12	160	$3200
Total Revenue from Merchandise Over the Year		$23,200

This projection assumes a steady increase in t-shirt sales each month as the book's popularity grows. The real figures will depend on various factors including the quality of the merchandise, how well it's promoted, the size of your fanbase, etc.

ONLINE COURSE

Ah, selling online courses - the digital equivalent of running a lemonade stand, but instead of lemonade, you're peddling your knowledge and instead of your neighbors, your customers could be anywhere in the world. It's just like inviting people into your brain and charging them for the privilege. The catch?

You've got to convince them your brain is worth the price of admission. And then there's the fun part of filming yourself talking for hours on end. You'll learn new skills you never thought you'd need, like video editing and realizing just how many "umms" and "ahhs" you can fit into a single sentence. Ah, the joys of monetizing wisdom!

SCENARIO 1: Assuming your online course is priced at $200 and you're starting with an established audience:

Month	Number of Courses Sold	Revenue
1	20	$4,000
2	30	$6,000
3	40	$8,000
4	50	$10,000
5	60	$12,000
6	70	$14,000
7	80	$16,000
8	90	$18,000
9	100	$20,000
10	110	$22,000
11	120	$24,000
12	130	$26,000
Total Revenue from the Online Course Over the Year		**$156,000**

Please note this is an optimistic projection and it assumes that you already have an engaged audience who is interested in your course, and that your marketing efforts are effective in continuously attracting new customers. Also, don't forget to subtract any costs related to producing and hosting the course, as well as transaction fees.

SCENARIO 2: Sell your online course for $497. Month 1 you sell 20 and go up by 10 for each month

Month	Number of Courses Sold	Price per Course	Revenue
1	20	$497	$9,940
2	30	$497	$14,910
3	40	$497	$19,880
4	50	$497	$24,850
5	60	$497	$29,820
6	70	$497	$34,790
7	80	$497	$39,760
8	90	$497	$44,730
9	100	$497	$49,700
10	110	$497	$54,670
11	120	$497	$59,640
12	130	$497	$64,610
Total Revenue:			**$446,500**

Remember, this is a projection and actual sales could be higher or lower depending on various factors including your marketing efforts, the value of your course, competition, and other factors. Also, the costs of creating, hosting, and marketing the course are not included in this projection.

31 UNIQUE WAYS TO MONETIZE YOUR BOOK

WHICH ONES ARE YOU GOING TO IMPLEMENT?

PRIORITIZE THEM INTO 4 CATEGORIES

1 - ABSOLUTELY WANT TO DO ASAP

2 - WANT TO DO WITHIN 1-3 MONTHS

3 - WANT TO DO IN 3-6 MONTHS

4 - WANT TO DO IN 6-12 MONTHS

5 - WANT TO DO SOMETIME IN THE FUTURE

MODULE	PRIORITY	COMPLETED BY
Module 3: The Power of Self-Publishing		
Module 4: Building Your Author Platform		
Module 5: Mastering the Art of Pre-orders		
Module 6: Transforming Your Book into an Audio Delight		
Module 7: Delving into Direct Sales		
Module 8: Navigating the Merchandising Maze		
Module 9: The Enchanting Realm of Repurposing Content		
Module 10: Profiting with Print-on-Demand		
Module 11: Leaning into Online Courses		
Module 12: The Magic of Licensing		
Module 13: Profiting from Public Speaking		
Module 14: The Allure of Affiliate Marketing		
Module 15: The Charm of Consulting and Coaching		
Module 16: Leveraging Your Network for Paid Appearances		
Module 17: Cashing In With Patreon and Crowdfunding		

Module 18: Making Sense of Sponsored Content		
Module 19: Building a Money-Making Membership Site		
Module 20: Cashing In on Advertising Revenue		
Module 21: The Globe-Trotting Adventures of Selling Foreign Rights		
Module 22: The Bundle of Joy: Book Bundling		
Module 23: Social Media, Your Golden Goose		
Module 24: Making Money the Generous Way: Donations and Tip Jars		
Module 25: Ghostwriting and Freelancing - Your Path to Extra Income		
Module 26: Leveraging Your Way to More Money		
Module 27: Lights, Camera, YouTube - Profiting from Videos		
Module 28: The Magic of Writing Sequels		
Module 29: Comparable Services, or the Art of Not Selling the Brooklyn Bridge		
Module 30: Leveraging Email Marketing: Making Money from the Inbox		
Module 31: Hosting Paid Live Events: Give Your Readers a Real-World Experience		

NEXT STEPS

Imagine turning each page of your book into a potential revenue stream with the '31 Unique Ways to Monetize Your Book' audio course!

Just at $497, this engaging and comprehensive course is your next step on the path to transforming your literary passion into a profitable venture.

Uncover the secrets of successful book monetization, learn innovative strategies to boost your earnings, and explore unique methods to engage your audience—all within the reach of your headphones.

It's not just a course, it's an investment in your future as a thriving author!

31 UNIQUE WAYS TO MONETIZE YOUR BOOK AUDIO COURSE $497

https://app.hiro.fm/channel/monetize

Unleash Your Author Potential: Exclusive Consultation with Bestselling Author Strategist, Kelly Falardeau

Don't miss this golden opportunity to engage with Kelly Falardeau, bestselling author strategist, in a power-packed hour-long consultation call for $497, where you'll dive deep into the thrilling world of books and explore five pivotal topics:

1) Unleashing your unique author's voice;

2) Mastering the art of strategic book planning;

3) Navigating the labyrinth of book publishing;

4) Harnessing the power of impactful book marketing, and

5) The ins-and-outs of becoming a bestseller - a transformative journey into the heart of authorship awaits you!

Schedule your call today for $497 at: https://bookkelly.as.me/consult